ART · FROM · THE · PAST

The ROMANS

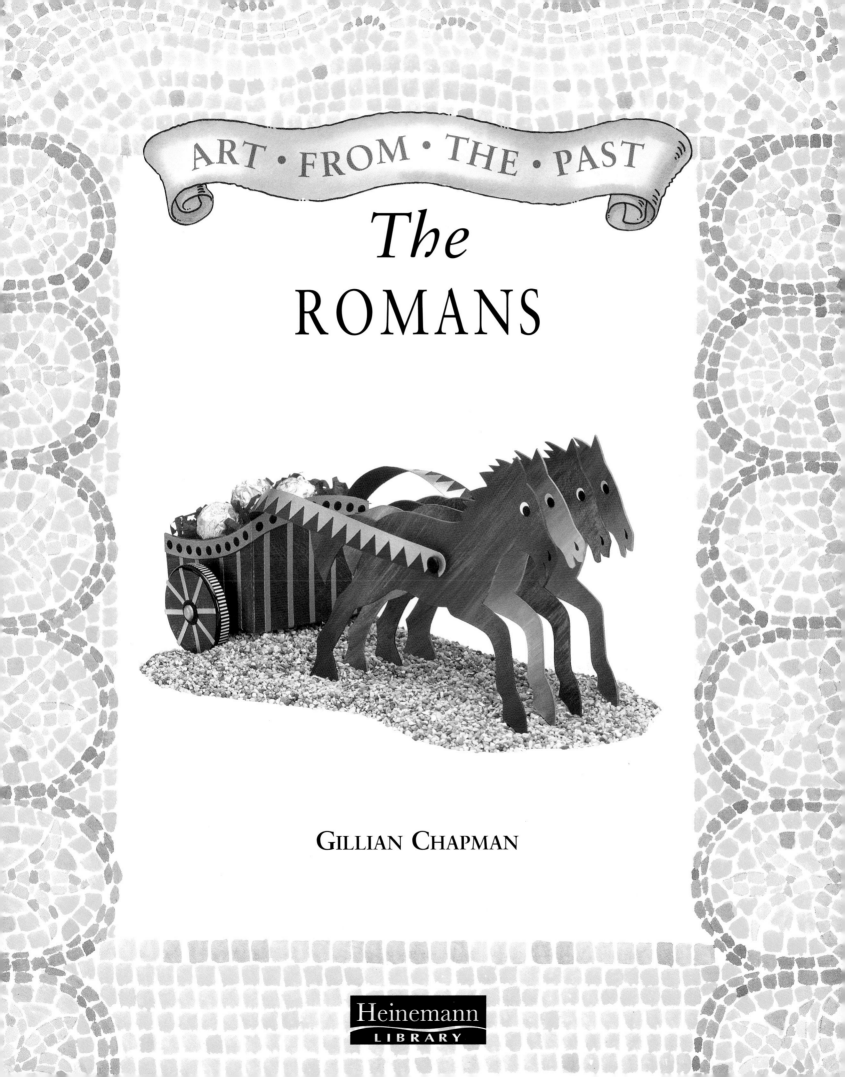

GILLIAN CHAPMAN

Heinemann LIBRARY

GENERAL CRAFT TIPS AND SAFETY PRECAUTIONS

Read the instructions carefully first then collect together everything you need
before you start work.

It helps to plan your design out first on rough paper.

If you are working with papier mâché or paint, cover the work surfaces
with newspaper.

Always use a cutting mat when cutting with a craft knife and ask
an adult to help if you are using sharp tools.

Keep paint and glue brushes separate and always wash them out after use.
Use non-toxic paints and glue.

Don't be impatient - make sure plaster is set, and papier mâché and paint
are thoroughly dry before moving on to the next stage!

All projects make perfect presents!
Try to make them as carefully as you can.

RECYCLING

Start collecting materials for craftwork. Save newspaper, clean coloured
paper and card, cardboard boxes and tubes of different sizes, glossy paper
and gift wrap, and scraps of string and ribbon.

Clean plastic containers and old utensils are perfect for mixing
plaster and making paper pulp.

PICTURE CREDITS

AKG Photos: 26; British Museum: 10, 16, 24, 34; C M Dixon: 6 bottom right, 8 top right, 12, 14, 22;
e.t. archive: 28; Michael Holford: 6 bottom left, 7 bottom left and right, 8 bottom right, 32;
Robert Harding: /Roy Rainford: 7 top left; SCALA: 8 bottom left; Werner Forman Archive:
/Museo Nazionale Romano, Rome 6 top left, 18, 20, 30, 36.

ART FROM THE PAST: THE ROMANS was produced by
Fernleigh Books, 61A Southbury Road, Enfield, Middlesex, EN1 1PJ.

Designers: Gillian Chapman and Gail Rose
Photographer: Rupert Horrox
Illustrator: Teri Gower Picture Researcher: Jennie Karrach

First published in Great Britain in 1998 by Heinemann Library,
an imprint of Heinemann Educational Publishers,
Halley Court, Jordan Hill, Oxford OX2 8EJ,
a division of Reed Educational and Professional Publishing Ltd.

Heinemann is a registered trademark of Reed Educational
& Professional Publishing Limited.

OXFORD MADRID ATHENS FLORENCE PRAGUE WARSAW
PORTSMOUTH NH CHICAGO SAO PAULO MEXICO CITY
SINGAPORE TOKYO MELBOURNE AUCKLAND KUALA LUMPUR
IBADAN GABORONE JOHANNESBURG KAMPALA NAIROBI

© Fernleigh Books 1998

British Library Cataloguing in Publication Data
Chapman, Gillian
The Romans. - (Art from the past)
1.Handicraft - Juvenile literature 2.Art, Roman - Juvenile literature
3.Imitation in art - Juvenile literature
I.Title
745.5'0937

ISBN 0 431 08064 X (Hardback)   ISBN 0 431 08066 6 (Paperback)

Printed in Hong Kong

The author and Fernleigh would like to thank
Keith Chapman for all his help with the model making.

ART · FROM · THE · PAST

The ROMANS

Gillian Chapman

THE ROMAN EMPIRE

ABOVE. *Roman soldiers in battle.*

BELOW. *The Roman **Forum** was the seat of government.*

IN THE 8TH CENTURY BC, Rome was a small farming community, situated on seven hills overlooking the river Tiber. It soon developed into one of the most powerful cities of all time. At first the small town of Rome was governed by the **Etruscans**, who ruled over central Italy, but noble Roman families overpowered the Etruscan kings and set up their own form of elected government. This marked the beginning of the Roman Republic in 509 BC.

The descendants of these noble families, known as **patricians**, continued to rule Rome as senators and elected politicians for hundreds of years, until the Republic fell into civil war. Eventually, a new system of rule and order was restored with an emperor in control. **Augustus** was the first Roman emperor and Rome was ruled peacefully by a succession of **emperors** for the next 400 years.

ABOVE. *Augustus ruled Rome from 27 BC to AD 14.*

THE POWER OF THE EMPIRE

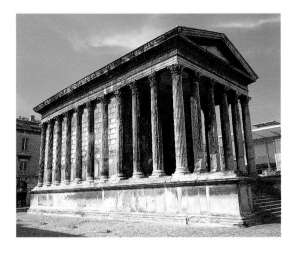

ABOVE. A *Roman temple in Nimes, France.*

BELOW: *The Pont du Gard, a Roman **aqueduct**, in Provence, France. It was three-stories high!*

THE ROMAN EMPIRE stretched over most of Europe, **Asia Minor** and North Africa. It was linked by a network of roads, bridges and aqueducts. After the army had conquered an area, the Romans would install a governor to keep the peace. Although they respected the customs of the people, the Romans were quick to leave their mark. They instigated huge building programmes throughout the empire, using local slave labour.

Roman architects and engineers were greatly influenced by Greek architecture, but they wanted to build bigger and better buildings. They used concrete, which was cheaper and more versatile than stone, to build grand structures. These were then covered with brick, plaster or marble.

BELOW. *The ruined **Colosseum** in Rome was built for **gladiator** fights.*

ROMAN CULTURE

THE ROMANS admired Greek culture. All Roman art, sculpture and literature shows the influence of the Greeks, but the Romans had a very different character. The Romans admired 'gravitas', which means strength and dignity, and perfectly describes the Roman personality. They portrayed themselves in a serious, dignified style.

Despite this portrayal of noble dignitaries, much of Roman society, business and politics was corrupt and led by ambitious emperors who wasted public funds on huge **amphitheatres** and circuses. During the 3rd century AD Roman generals began competing for power. Civil war, together with invasions along its vast borders, caused the Empire to decline. In AD 324, the **Emperor** Constantine built a new capital at Byzantium, renaming it Constantinople. This led to further division within the Empire and the eventual fall of Rome.

ABOVE. This statue of a **senator** shows the typical serious Roman style of sculpture.

BELOW RIGHT. Coin of Nero, one of the most corrupt of the Roman Emperors. He murdered his mother and his wife.

BELOW. Marble **relief** of chariot racing at the **Circus Maximus**.

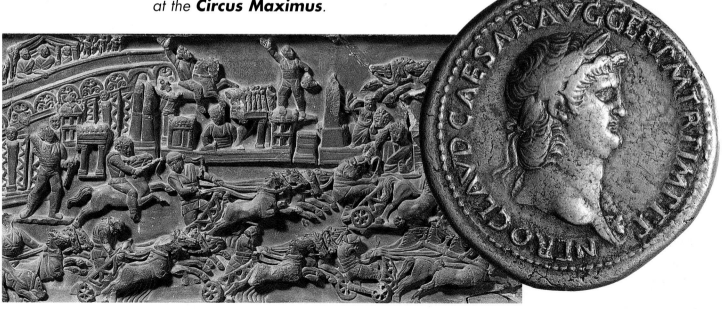

ROMAN CRAFT TIPS

The Romans were great builders and some projects involve making buildings and columns. Gluing tissue onto old boxes and card gives them a rough texture that looks like stonework.

Columns can be made by covering card tubes with corrugated paper or drinking straws. Both ways look convincing. Cover the straws with the tissue before painting.

Paint columns and buildings to look like marble or stone. Dab on thick grey and beige paint with a large brush. Don't forget to paint in some cracks and pieces of ivy.

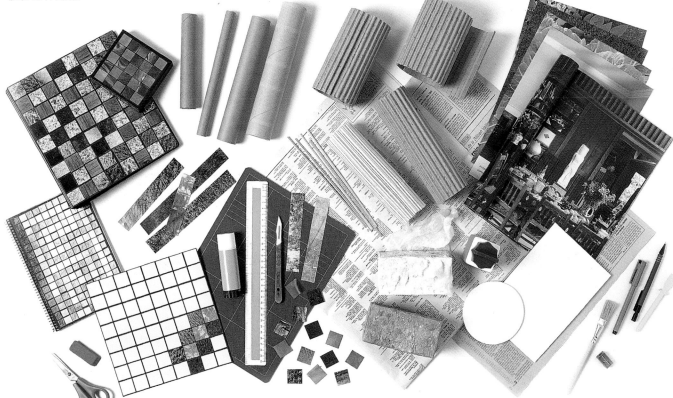

The Romans decorated their homes with mosaics and so can you. First draw a grid of squares with a black felt pen. Then colour in the squares with felt pens or squares of coloured paper.

Collect old magazines and cut out mosaic squares from the pages. It is a cheap and easy way of finding all the colours you need for your mosaic picture. Glue the squares down with a glue stick.

Some projects suggest using thick card as a base or for part of the structure. Try using foam board instead. It is easy to buy from craft shops and is much easier to cut and shape than thick card.

MAKING MOSAICS

THE ROMANS made spectacular mosaic pictures from small pieces of stone, or 'tesserae'. Craftspeople laid coloured cubes of white chalk, **terracotta**, blue or black slate and yellow sandstone into wet cement.

Mosaics were used extensively to pave public buildings, but only the rich could afford them in their **villas**. Mosaic factories in Italy and **Gaul** produced catalogues of their designs, ranging from cheap border patterns to very expensive scenes from literature and **mythology**.

Many Roman mosaics are in perfect condition today, like the patterned floor panel above, that was made in AD 100.

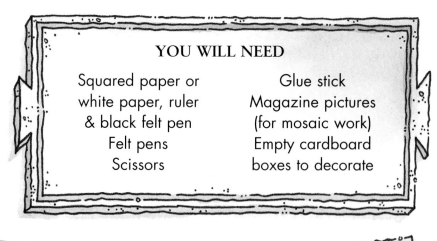

YOU WILL NEED

Squared paper or white paper, ruler & black felt pen	Glue stick
Felt pens	Magazine pictures (for mosaic work)
Scissors	Empty cardboard boxes to decorate

BORDER PATTERNS

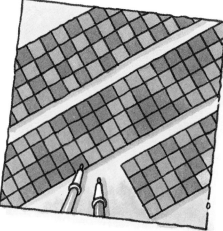

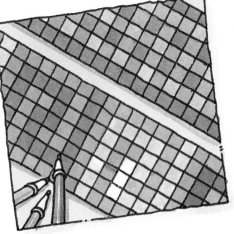

1. Use either the squared paper to design your mosaic patterns or draw your own grid by dividing white paper into 1 cm squares.

2. Cut a 4 cm by 30 cm strip of squared paper and make a two-colour pattern by colouring in alternate squares. Start with simple step designs.

3. Try making up your own designs using wider strips of paper, with 3 or 4 colours. The designs shown above are often used in Roman mosaics.

SQUARE DESIGNS

Use natural colours in your mosaic designs and transform cardboard boxes into stunning mosaic gift boxes.

1. Cut out a grid measuring 5 or 6 cm square and experiment with different designs. How many different patterns can you make?

2. Try using squares of different sizes. Divide the small squares in half to form triangles and include these in the design to make these 'arrow' patterns.

3. Cut up scraps of coloured paper into 1 cm squares and, following your colour scheme, glue them to your design for a really bold mosaic effect!

MOSAIC GAMES

SOME WEALTHY FAMILIES had baths in their homes, but most Romans went to the public baths to relax. The Romans loved to play games and the baths were an important place to exercise and socialise. Some men played ball games, wrestled or trained with weights, while others preferred less energetic games. They sat with friends enjoying a board game or gambling with dice.

Our modern game of Ludo takes its name from the Latin word 'ludi' meaning game. Use mosaic patterns to decorate these Roman board games.

YOU WILL NEED

Paper & black felt pen (or squared paper)
Ruler & scissors
Felt pens
Cardboard
Coloured sticky tape

Craft knife & cutting mat
Glue stick
Magazine pictures for mosaic work
Checkers or games counters & dice

CHECKER BOARD

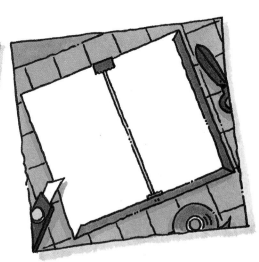

1. First you will need to plan the board design on paper. The checker board has eight squares on each side, plus a border. Work out the measurements accurately.

2. Measure the size of the board design. Then cut out a square of cardboard so that when the board design is placed on top there is a 1cm gap left all around the edge.

3. Cut the cardboard square in half. Tape the two halves together, so the board can be folded. Tape the sides of the board to strengthen it and tidy up all the edges.

4. Now you can finish the checker board mosaic. Cut the scraps of coloured paper to size and glue them over the paper design. Use the ideas on pages 9-11 to make the border patterns.

5. Make sure all the mosaic pieces are glued down, then carefully fold the paper in half to make a central crease. Align the crease with the centre fold of the board and glue in place.

Design a matching box to keep the checker board and counters in.

Try designing other games. Draughts and Ludo are traditional games, but you may like to invent a board game of your own.

SCRIBES AND SCROLLS

THE ROMANS introduced the Latin alphabet to western Europe where it is still in use today. However 2,000 years ago, most Romans were illiterate and only the well-educated could read.

The vast Roman administration needed **scribes** to keep records. They wrote on wax tablets, scratching the surface with a **stylus**. It is believed that the speeches of the great Roman emperors and senators were recorded in this way. Permanent records would be transcribed in ink onto papyrus scrolls or **vellum**.

The lady above is holding a wax tablet and stylus, and the man has a **papyrus** scroll. Written scrolls were the Roman equivalent of books.

PAPYRUS SCROLL

YOU WILL NEED

Thick card or foam board
Ruler & scissors
Craft knife & cutting mat
Pair of compasses
Length of dowel
Drawing pins

PVA glue & brush
Papyrus or paper
Paints & brush
Sticky tape
Card tube & split pins
Scraps of ribbon

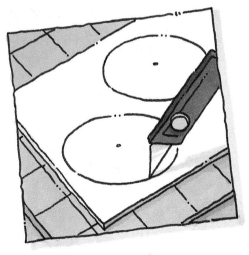

1. Use a pair of compasses to draw two 6 cm circles on the thick card. Then cut the circles out carefully using the craft knife on the cutting mat.

2. Use a compass point to enlarge the hole in the centre of the circles. Attach to each end of the dowel with drawing pins. Ask an adult to help.

3. Draw two 4 cm and two 2.5 cm circles on the card and cut them out carefully. Use the PVA to glue them onto the larger circle.

4. Wait for the glue to dry, making sure the card circles are firmly secure. Then paint the scroll and decorate the ends with scraps of ribbon.

5. Cut a length of papyrus slightly narrower than the dowel. Write the inscription first before attaching it to the scroll with sticky tape.

6. Make a case for the scroll from a card tube. Paint the tube and decorate it with mosaic patterns (see page 10). Attach a card handle with split pins.

Make your scrolls look more authentic by copying a Latin inscription on them.

ROMAN TIME

THE EMPEROR **Julius Caesar** organised the Roman calendar into 12 months. We still use this calendar today. Many of the months were named after gods and **emperors**. January and March were named after the Roman gods **Janus** and Mars, July and August were named after the Emperors **Julius** and **Augustus**.

The Romans also divided the day into hours. They used letters to represent a number – I is 1, V is 5 and X is 10. These numerals are still used on modern watches and clocks.

Circular picture mosaics were often used to decorate walls and pavements. They make perfect designs for a Roman clock face.

MOSAIC CLOCK

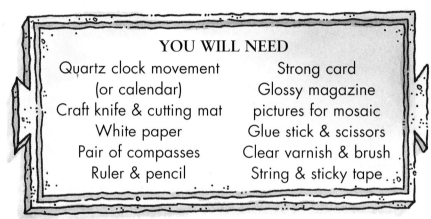

YOU WILL NEED

Quartz clock movement (or calendar)
Craft knife & cutting mat
White paper
Pair of compasses
Ruler & pencil

Strong card
Glossy magazine pictures for mosaic
Glue stick & scissors
Clear varnish & brush
String & sticky tape

1. The diameter of your clock face will depend on the length of the hands of your quartz movement, but 25 cm is a good size. Draw a 25 cm circle on the paper.

2. Design your clock face using ideas from the mosaic pavement design shown above. Include the numerals in your design and make sure they are correct!

3. Carefully cut out a 25 cm circle from a sheet of strong card using the craft knife. Transfer the outline of your design onto the card and pencil in the details.

6. Tape a small length of string securely to the back of the mosaic and hang it on the wall.

If you do not have a quartz movement, make the mosaic face and hang a calendar underneath.

4. Cut small mosaic pieces from coloured magazine pictures. Choose colours to suit your design. Follow the outlines and glue the pieces in place.

5. Coat the mosaic with clear varnish. This will help to protect the picture. Make a hole in the centre and ask an adult to help you install the quartz movement.

The clock face is a circular design with curves, so don't make all the mosaic pieces square.

CLASSIC COLUMNS

THE ROMANS were great architects and engineers, who built on a grand scale. They used columns, arches, vaults and domes carved from marble and stone, to build magnificent **amphitheatres**, temples, **aqueducts** and bridges. Many are still standing today.

The Romans used columns in the traditional Greek styles, but also developed new types of column tops called capitals, which are still used by architects.

Try making this picture frame with its classical Roman columns. It's impressive enough to frame the portrait of the noble Roman Emperor Hadrian!

COLUMN FRAME

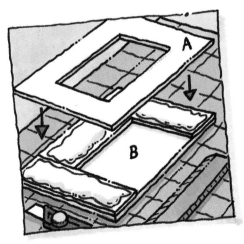

1. Draw a 3.5cm border on card A and cut out the centre with a craft knife. Glue 3cm wide card strips to three sides of card B. Cover the strips with glue and stick the cards together.

2. Cut lengths of card and glue them to the bottom of the frame to make steps. Cut a triangle of card for the roof, glue it to the top and trim off any surplus corners of card.

3. Cut the drinking straws to size and glue them to the sides of the frame to make the columns. Glue the button and the cocktail sticks to the roof to make the decorative frieze.

Paint the columns to look like marble. The tissue paper will give the frame a cracked texture.

4. Tear up small pieces of white tissue and using a diluted mix of PVA, cover the frame with several layers. Make sure the tissue covers all the dents and grooves.

5. Dip lengths of string into the glue and shape them into coils to decorate the tops of the columns. Glue a strip of corrugated card to the roof to look like roof tiles.

6. To make the frame stand up, cut a triangle of card, score and fold it along one side and glue the fold to the back. Then paint the frame to look like marble.

TEMPLES AND SHRINES

THE ROMANS worshiped many different gods. Each god was associated with healing the sick or granting success in battle or business. Sacrifices were made to the gods when their help was needed.

Most Roman households had a small shrine where the family could offer prayers and gifts of food or flowers to their favourite gods, and also remember the spirits of their ancestors.

Snakes were often painted on shrines, such as on this one in the House of Vetii in Italy. The Romans believed that the snake's spirit protected the family.

YOU WILL NEED

Two empty cardboard boxes (cereal boxes are ideal)
Sticky tape
Scraps of thick card
Craft knife & cutting mat
Pencil & ruler

PVA glue & brush
Four cardboard tubes
Corrugated paper
Scissors
Poster paints & brush
Two split pins
Newspaper

TEMPLE GIFT BOX

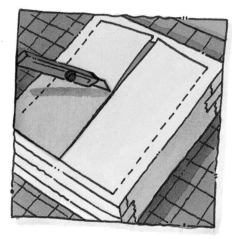

1. Tape over the opening flaps at the top and bottom of both of the empty boxes. Draw a rectangle on the front of one box, 15 mm in from the edge, and divide it in half.

2. The lines show the position of the opening doors. Cut along them carefully with a craft knife. Do not cut along the dotted lines as these will form the door hinges.

3. Cut two pieces of thick card about 6 cm larger than the base of the box. Glue the box to one of the pieces with PVA. The second piece will be used for the roof.

4. Cut the four tubes to the same height as the box and cover them in corrugated paper. Position a tube at each corner of the box, gluing them in place with the PVA glue.

5. Cut a triangular section from the second box to make a roof shape that will fit on the second piece of card. Make sure the base of the roof is the same length as the card.

6. Tape the roof shape to the card and glue the roof to the top of the box. Cut a strip of corrugated paper and glue it to the roof. Paint the box and attach the split pins to the doors.

Make some shelves or dividers for the gift boxes from strips of card glued into position.

Fill the temple boxes with gifts of sweets, stationary or even soaps for a Roman bath!

MARBLE STATUES

GRAND PUBLIC BUILDINGS and temples were built by the Romans to show how important and powerful they were. These structures were filled with huge statues and carved **reliefs** in honour of Roman gods and **emperors**. The Altar of Peace erected by the Emperor **Augustus** in 13 BC contains marble statues (left).

Italian quarries provided the sculptors with a plentiful supply of high quality marble. All statues and portraits were extremely realistic, showing every feature and detail, with great pose and calm expressions of dignity.

Try casting your own piece of sculpture to use as a handy paperweight!

PLASTER PAPERWEIGHT

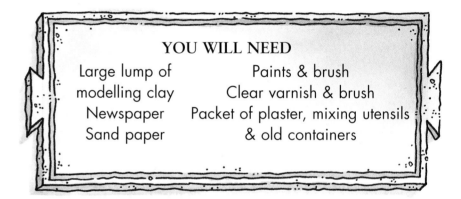

YOU WILL NEED

Large lump of modelling clay	Paints & brush
Newspaper	Clear varnish & brush
Sand paper	Packet of plaster, mixing utensils & old containers

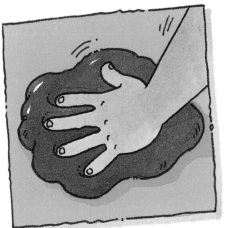

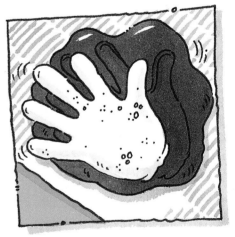

1. Take a large lump of modelling clay and soften it by kneading it with your hands. Press your open hand into the clay, pushing all your fingers in as far as possible.

2. Spread newspaper over the work surface. Using old utensils, mix up the plaster following the instructions on the packet. Then pour the plaster into the clay mould.

3. Leave the plaster to set. When it is dry, carefully peel away the clay mould. Parts of the plaster hand may still be slightly damp, so leave it in a safe place to dry out.

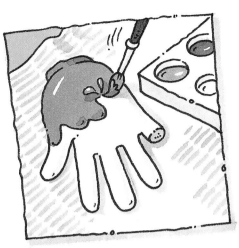

4. Only when the hand is completely dry can you begin to rub down any unwanted cracks and lumps of plaster with sand paper.

5. Don't worry if part of a finger breaks off accidentally, or if you lose a thumb – it will just makes the cast look more old and authentic!

6. Finally paint the hand paperweight in the colours of natural marble and leave to dry. Two coats of clear varnish will help to protect it.

Use the hand paperweight to hold paper clips and drawing pins!

Experiment with making other plaster paperweights. Try taking a plaster cast of your toes!

TERRACOTTA LAMPS

ROMAN HOMES were lit with oil lamps made from **terracotta** or bronze. Each lamp was filled with olive oil and a wick was placed in the nozzle and lit. Because olive oil was expensive people tended to go to bed when it got dark outside.

Some Roman lamps were very elaborate and had several nozzles – many wicks gave a brighter light. Others were beautifully carved by lamp makers with scenes from **mythology** and everyday life. The intricate carvings on the lamps provide us with tiny illustrations of Roman life.

This terracotta lamp shows a chariot race at the **Circus Maximus** in Rome (see page 32). It includes details of the spectators, the starting gates and the chariots.

One example shows details of the harbour at Carthage, with fishermen in boats casting their nets. It was made by the lampmaker Augendus in AD 200.

CANDLE LAMP

1. Soften the self-hardening clay in your hands. Then roll it out on a board with a rolling pin until it is about 1cm thick. Use a large pastry cutter to cut out a circle of clay.

2. The clay circle will form the base of the lamp. Place the night light in the centre of the base. Build up the lamp shape around the night light with small pieces of clay.

3. Keep adding the clay until it is level with the top of the night light. Use your fingers to flatten the top and shape the sides of the lamp, giving the lamp a curved shape.

*The clay lamps can be left
as a natural terracotta finish,
or painted to look like bronze.*

*These candle lamps are very
pretty, but could become dangerous.
NEVER leave them unattended.*

4. Use a wet sponge to keep the clay damp and to smooth over all the surfaces. Roll out a length of clay into a sausage shape that is long enough to make the handle.

5. Wet the side of the lamp and attach the handle. Curve it into shape and smooth over the join where it is attached to the side of the lamp. Finally smooth over all the surfaces.

6. Use the wooden sticks to decorate the lamp with a simple pattern. Then leave the lamp in a safe place and let the clay harden before painting and varnishing.

EMPERORS AND RULERS

THE FIRST ROMAN EMPERORS refused to wear crowns because they did not want to be thought of as kings, so they wore laurel wreaths. Purple was an expensive dye so **emperors** wore **togas** dyed purple as a symbol of their status. It became treason for anyone else to wear a purple toga.

Many modern states have political and legal systems based on the Roman model of government. The American Constitution adopted many Roman ideas, and words like '**senate**' and 'republic' are all Roman.

This is a bust of the most famous Roman ruler and general, **Julius Caesar**.

YOU WILL NEED

Wide card tube	Newspaper
Corrugated card	Two large bowls
Corrugated paper	PVA glue & brush
Scissors	Poster paints & brush
Sticky tape	Bay leaves/green paper

IMPERIAL BUST

1. Cut out several squares of corrugated card slightly larger than the diameter of the card tube. Glue them all together and then glue them to the top of the tube with PVA.

2. Cut a length of corrugated paper the same width as the tube and use it to cover the tube. Make sure there is enough paper to overlap at the back, then glue it in place.

3. Scrunch up a ball of newspaper until it is large enough for the head. Tape it together firmly. Then secure it to the top of the plinth with lengths of sticky tape.

5. Press the lumps of pulp to the newspaper head and work all the way round, building up the head shape.

Try making a wreath from bay leaves or green paper to crown the bust.

4. Soak pieces of newspaper in warm water. Then squeeze the water out and mash the paper in another bowl with the PVA to make pulp.

6. Brush on extra PVA to help the pulp stick to the head. Add extra pulp and model it with your fingers to shape the features.

Take your time to get the head to look right, then allow the pulp to completely dry before painting.

Make a bust of someone you know. Ask them to pose for you. When you have finished, paint the bust to look like stone or marble.

ROMAN COINS

Coins were originally minted in Rome as a method of paying soldiers wages and collecting taxes. During the reign of the Emperor **Augustus**, coins were given a fixed value. Copper coins were worth less than bronze, silver and gold coins. The same coins were used throughout the Empire to make trading easier.

As the Roman Empire expanded, communication was difficult. Coins were used to spread information and propaganda.

Like the Roman Emperors, try minting your own coins to mark an important event or celebration.

CELEBRATION COIN

YOU WILL NEED

Strip of corrugated card	Scissors & ruler
Paper clip	Paint brush
Modelling clay	Plaster
Board & rolling pin	Newspaper
Old plastic containers & mixing utensils	Poster paints in metallic colours

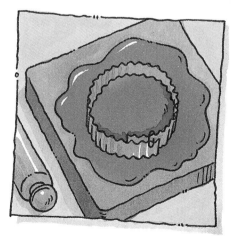

1. Cut a strip of corrugated card and fix it into a circular shape with a paper clip. The strip length will determine the size of the coin.

2. Roll out the modelling clay on a board until it is smooth and flat. Push the corrugated card into the clay, keeping the circular shape.

3. Use old plastic or wooden tools to make patterns and designs in the surface of the clay. These will be the markings on the coin.

4. Follow the instructions on the packet to mix up a small amount of plaster. Always use old plastic containers and utensils when making plaster.

5. Pour the plaster into the coin mould to a depth of about 2 cm. Smooth the surface of the plaster and leave it to dry in a safe place.

6. Remove the plaster coin from the clay mould and peel away the corrugated strip. Now the coin is ready to paint in metallic poster paints.

Make a series of coins and paint them in different metallic paints.

Why not make a blank plaster coin and scratch out a design on the smooth surface using wooden carving tools.

BATTLING GLADIATORS

THE **AMPHITHEATRE** was a public arena where performances and games were held. During festivals huge crowds could watch **gladiator** fights, wild beast hunts and even executions. These events were very violent and thousands of people and animals were killed to entertain the crowds.

Gladiators were prisoners and slaves who were trained to fight with all different types of weapons, including swords, tridents and even nets. Some survived, became popular with the crowds and won their freedom.

Exotic animals, such as lions, panthers and bears, were hunted down and brought to the arenas from all parts of the Empire to fight the gladiators.

GLADIATOR SWORD FIGHT

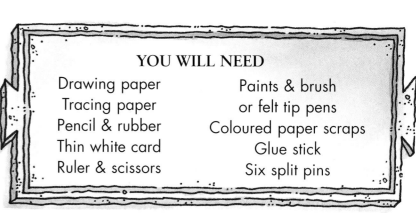

YOU WILL NEED

Drawing paper
Tracing paper
Pencil & rubber
Thin white card
Ruler & scissors

Paints & brush
or felt tip pens
Coloured paper scraps
Glue stick
Six split pins

1. Make a drawing of two gladiators fighting. Keep the body shapes simple, but draw in all the details of the helmets, shields and armour.

2. When you are happy with your drawing, trace the top part onto a piece of thin card. Include all the details, except for the legs.

3. Trace the legs onto the card. They will be cut out separately. Draw over all the traced lines. Make the legs 2 cm longer than the drawing.

By holding the main drawing and moving the leg support from side to side the gladiators will appear to fight!

4. Colour in your drawing using paints or felt pens, or make a collage design with scraps of coloured paper glued into place.

5. Carefully cut out the main drawing. Cut close to the lines, but do not worry about cutting around all the small details. Cut out the four legs.

6. Attach the legs to the bodies with split pins. Then attach the outer leg of each gladiator to another length of card using split pins.

CHARIOT RACING

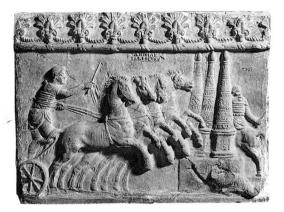

CHARIOT RACING was an exciting occasion that all the family enjoyed. In Rome, the event was held at a huge race track called the **Circus Maximus**. It was an extremely dangerous sport. Chariots were light-weight, built for speed and usually pulled by a team of four horses called a quadriga.

There were many fatal accidents, especially on the bends, but victorious **charioteers** became great public heroes.

A white flag signalled the start, huge starting gates opened and up to twelve chariots raced around the oval track.

CHARIOT AND HORSES

YOU WILL NEED
Small cardboard box	Tracing paper
Scraps of coloured card	Stiff card
Sharp pencil	Poster paints & brush
Scissors & Glue stick	Two lids the same size
Drawing pins	Two 12 cm dowels

Ask an adult to help you to make the wheels.

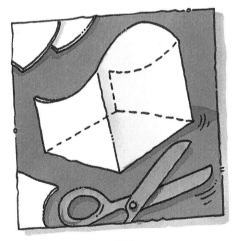

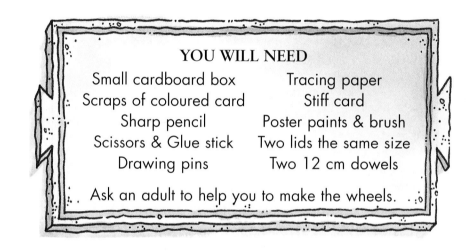

1. To make the chariot body, take the cardboard box and cut it into a chariot shape (above). Cut off the back and curve the sides and front.

2. Use a sharp pencil to make a hole in either side of the box. Make sure the two holes line up so the axle for the wheels will thread through.

3. Cut out two circles of card and glue them to the lids. Either paint the chariot body and wheels or decorate them with scraps of coloured card.

4. Draw an outline of a galloping horse on tracing paper. Trace the horse onto card four times and cut them out. Either paint the horses or use different coloured card.

5. Carefully push a drawing pin through the centre of the lids and attach a lid to one end of the dowel. Pass it through the chariot's body and attach the second lid.

6. Use the sharp pencil to make a hole through the body of each horse. Make sure all the holes line up, then pass the second dowel through all the holes.

7. Cut two strips of card to make reins. Glue one end of each to the chariot and attach the other end to the dowel with a drawing pin.

Try making several teams of chariots and horses, and race them in your own Circus Maximus!

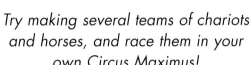

Fill the chariots with sweets or small gifts.

WEAPONS OF WAR

The Roman army was a strong, disciplined force, led by skilled generals, like **Julius Caesar**. Soldiers were well-armed and well-trained, and were supported by teams of craftsmen, who built bridges, weapons and camp sites.

When attacking a heavily defended town, tall siege towers were built near the battle site and pushed into position by teams of men and horses. Huge catapults were made to hurl rocks and burning objects over the walls.

Groups of soldiers in formation used their shields as protection against the enemy.

SIEGE TOWER PERISCOPE

YOU WILL NEED

Stiff card
Ruler & pencil
Sticky tape & scissors
Single hole punch
Craft knife & cutting mat

Two small mirrors
PVA glue & brush
Four small plastic lids
Kebab sticks
Lolly sticks

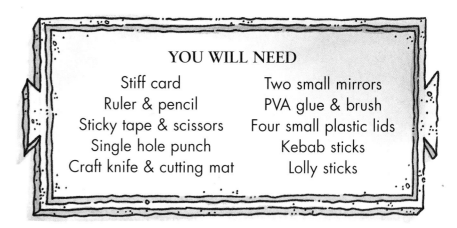

1. Cut out a piece of card, 30 by 34 cm. Divide it into sections, each 8 cm wide, leaving a 2 cm flap. Cut out two window shapes in the card, as shown.

2. Score along the lines, fold the box and tape it together along the flap edge. Cut out two lengths of card, each measuring 8 by 26 cm. Divide these into sections as shown.

3. Score along the lines, fold into the triangular shape and tape it together. Glue a mirror to the longest side using the PVA. Then make the second mirror support.

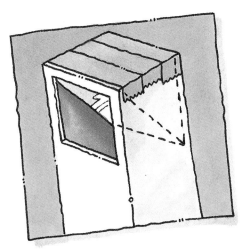

5. Cut out a 12 cm square of card, and cut it into shape. Punch two holes in the opposite flaps, making sure the holes line up. Score and fold the flaps and tape them together with sticky tape.

The shape of the siege tower makes a perfect periscope for you to spy on an enemy.

4. Position a mirror support in the top of the tower. The side of the support should form the top of the box. Tape it in place and position the second mirror in the base.

6. Glue the base to the **periscope**. Ask an adult to make a hole in the centre of each lid. Thread a length of kebab stick through the holes and glue a lid to each end.

Decorate the periscope with pieces of lolly stick.

Try designing a simple catapult. Make the wheel base, as explained in step 5. Construct the catapult with sections of card, dowel and an empty bottle lid.

ROMAN RUINS

OVER 1,500 YEARS after the decline of their Empire, the Romans still influence our modern lives. Roman roads were originally built for the army to use, but they soon became vital trade routes, linking major towns by the shortest distances. These routes still service many European cities.

As the Empire expanded, ruling emperors wanted to leave their mark. They erected grand buildings and triumphal arches as records of their conquests.

Some Roman buildings are still in use today, however many, like this Roman **Forum** in Italy, are just imposing ruins.

ROMAN RUIN DESK TIDY

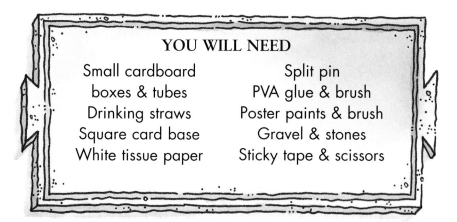

YOU WILL NEED
Small cardboard boxes & tubes	Split pin
Drinking straws	PVA glue & brush
Square card base	Poster paints & brush
White tissue paper	Gravel & stones
	Sticky tape & scissors

1. Gather together the empty cardboard boxes and tubes you have collected and arrange them on the card base. These will become the main parts of the Roman ruin.

2. Cut down the tubes if they are too tall. Then cut the straws to size and glue them to the tubes using PVA. Cover the tubes with glued pieces of white tissue paper.

3. If you have an empty chocolate box with a sliding drawer, make a handle in the drawer with a split pin. This will become a handy pencil or pen drawer.

4. Cut the lids off some of the small boxes and tape the sides together so they don't fall apart. Now stack up the boxes and arrange all the pieces again on the base.

5. When you are happy with the arrangement, glue all the pieces together with PVA. Cover the boxes with glued pieces of tissue and glue small stones to the base.

6. When the glue has dried, paint the ruined columns and masonry to look like marble. Don't forget to paint some cracks in the columns to make them look old.

This Roman ruin makes an impressive desk tidy.

GLOSSARY

Amphitheatre – a large arena with tiered seats so that thousands of spectators can watch the games.

Aqueducts – water channels, often raised above ground, that supplied a city with water.

Asia Minor – a large area of land that formed the eastern extent of the Roman Empire, know today as Turkey and Syria.

Augustus – the first emperor of Rome, who ruled between 27 BC and AD 14.

Charioteer – a chariot driver, usually a slave. Successful charioteers, like **gladiators**, became popular with the crowds and sometimes made enough profit to buy their freedom.

Circus Maximus – a huge race track in the centre of Rome, built for chariot racing.

It had seating for 45,000 spectators and underground cages for wild beasts. The main arena could be flooded to stage sea-battles.

Colosseum – the large **amphitheatre** in the centre of Rome built for **gladiator** fights.

Emperor – the ruler of Rome, who had great power over the army and the senate.

Etruscans – a race of people who lived in central Italy in Roman times.

Forum – the central market square of a city, often paved, and surrounded by important public buildings.

Gaul – the ancient name for the area known today as France.

Gladiators – slaves or prisoners that were trained to fight in the **amphitheatre** arenas.

Gravitas – Latin word meaning strength and dignity.

Janus – the Roman god whose name is given to the month of January. Janus had two faces – one looked back on the old year, the other looked forward to the new.

Julius Caesar – the most famous Roman ruler and general, who was assassinated in 44 BC.

Mythological – fictional stories about gods and heroes that have been retold through time.

Papyrus – a reed-like plant used to make paper.

Patrician – descendants of noble Roman families who ruled Rome as **senators** and politicians.

Periscope – a spying device first used during the American Civil War. It enabled soldiers to see the enemy by using mirrors, without putting themselves in danger.

Relief – a design that is raised above, or carved into, stone or marble.

Scribe – a professional writer and record keeper, who could read and write Latin script.

Senator – the elected rulers of Rome who debated at the Senate and made laws.

Stylus – a pointed writing tool, used to write on wax covered tablets.

Terracotta – word meaning 'burnt earth'. It is a form of red clay used for pottery.

Tesserae – small cubes of coloured stone, used to make mosaic pictures.

Toga – traditional loose robe worn by the Roman nobility.

Vellum – prepared animal skins, used for writing on and making scrolls.

Villa – the country mansion of a wealthy Roman family.